6/12

CR

ADRIAN PETERSON

BY MARTY GITLIN

Published by ABDO Publishing Company, PO Box 398166, Minneapolis, MN 55439. Copyright © 2012 by Abdo Consulting Group, Inc. International copyrights reserved in all countries. No part of this book may be reproduced in any form without written permission from the publisher. SportsZone™ is a trademark and logo of ABDO Publishing Company.

Printed in the United States of America,
North Mankato, Minnesota
092011
012012

 THIS BOOK CONTAINS AT LEAST 10% RECYCLED MATERIALS.

Editor: Chrös McDougall
Copy Editor: Anna Comstock
Series Design: Craig Hinton
Cover and Interior Production: Kazuko Collins

Photo Credits: David Drapkin/AP Images, cover, 1; Tom Olmscheid/AP Images, 4; Pablo Martinez Monsivais/AP Images, 7; David Branch/AP Images, 9; Donna McWilliam/AP Images, 10; Ronen Zilberman/AP Images, 13; Matt York/AP Images, 14; Frank Franklin II/AP Images, 17; Ed Zurga/AP Images, 18; M. Spencer Green/AP Images, 21; G. Newman Lowrance/AP Images, 23; Paul Sancya/AP Images, 24; Andy King/AP Images, 27; Denis Poroy/AP Images, 29

Library of Congress Cataloging-in-Publication Data
Gitlin, Marty.
  Adrian Peterson : record-setting running back / by Marty Gitlin.
    p. cm. — (Playmakers)
  Includes bibliographical references and index.
  ISBN 978-1-61783-293-2
  1. Peterson, Adrian—Juvenile literature. 2. Football players—United States—Biography—Juvenile literature. 3. Running backs (Football—United States—Biography—Juvenile literature. 4. Minnesota Vikings (Football team)—Juvenile literature. I. Title.
  GV939.P477G57 2012
  796.332092—dc23
  [B]
                              2011039418

TABLE OF CONTENTS

CHAPTER 1

RUNNING WILD

Adrian Peterson grabbed the football. He sprinted 64 yards into the end zone for a touchdown. The score allowed his team, the Minnesota Vikings, to tie the San Diego Chargers. And he was just warming up. Adrian ran 34 yards two drives later. That set up the go-ahead touchdown. Then he bolted 46 yards for another score. That sealed the Vikings' 35–17 victory. But Adrian was still not done. He added a 35-yard run to

Adrian Peterson hurdles a defender during his record-setting 2007 game against the San Diego Chargers.

put an exclamation point on one of the greatest performances in National Football League (NFL) history.

Adrian rushed for 296 yards that day in 2007. That was an NFL record. Adrian also scored three touchdowns in the game. Not bad for a rookie!

Becoming one of the NFL's top running backs was not easy. It was something Adrian dreamed about from a young age. He knew that he would have to work very hard to reach that goal. So that is what he did.

Adrian grew up in Palestine, Texas. He had lots of energy growing up. Adrian's father Nelson remembers his son often running around. So he nicknamed Adrian "A. D." That stands for "all day," because Adrian played sports all day. People still called Adrian that when he got to the NFL.

Adrian was a top football player at Palestine High School. He was also a star sprinter. The 100-meter dash was his best event. He even reached the finals at the state championships as a sophomore. His mother Bonita Jackson had also been a track star. She won four events at the Texas state track meet in 1983.

Adrian became the fifth NFL running back to rush for a combined 3,000 yards in his first two seasons.

Life was not always easy for Adrian. He was forced to deal with tragedy at age seven. One afternoon, he watched as a drunk driver killed his 11-year-old brother, Brian. Seven years later, Nelson was sent to jail. He had to leave his family for a 10-year prison sentence.

Those events were hard on Adrian. But he never let them take him down. Instead, he used them as motivation to make the most out of his own life. Adrian found his calling in sports. His favorite sport was football. He played running back at Palestine High School. Opponents had a hard time catching him. He was very fast and athletic.

Palestine is a small city in east Texas. There are many big college football teams in the surrounding areas. It did not take long for their coaches to hear of Adrian. He rushed for more than 2,000 yards as a junior in high school. And he added 22 touchdowns. Coaches from more than just Texas soon wanted him to play for their teams. Scholarship offers poured in from the nation's best college teams. Palestine coach Jeff Harrell once saw recruiters from three major schools arguing over who could see Adrian first.

Adrian finished his high school career on a high note. He rushed for 350 yards and six touchdowns in his final game.

Palestine High School football coach Jeff Harrell remembered seeing Adrian in practice for the first time. The young player blew away the coaches. "All the coaches just looked at each other as if to say, 'Did you just see what I saw?'" Harrell said.

Adrian smiles with his mother as he announces his decision to attend Oklahoma.

And that was just in the first half! Adrian ended the season with an incredible 2,960 rushing yards and 32 touchdowns.

Several top colleges hoped Adrian would choose to play for their teams next. Among them was the University of Texas. But Adrian decided to go north. He chose to play for the University of Oklahoma.

Adrian Peterson

SOONER STANDOUT

There is a big change from high school to college football. Only the very best high school players reach the college level. They are the biggest, strongest, and fastest athletes. So it often takes some time for college freshmen athletes to adjust. But Adrian Peterson was not the average freshman athlete.

The Oklahoma Sooners are almost always a top team. They were even national champions in 2000.

Peterson runs strong for the Oklahoma Sooners as a freshman in 2004.

Peterson joined the team in 2004. And he quickly became the starting running back. But that was just the beginning.

Peterson rushed for more than 100 yards in his first game. He kept running wild after that. He ran for more than 100 yards in 10 of the next 11 games. Peterson even had three games where he rushed for more than 200 yards. One of them was against Texas. That was Oklahoma's main rival. Peterson rushed for 1,925 yards that season. That was a national record for freshmen. He had become one of the greatest running backs in the country.

The Sooners finished the regular season with a perfect 12–0 record. Peterson got to play in the national championship game that year. However, Oklahoma lost to the University of Southern California.

Peterson and his dad Nelson Peterson pose for pictures at the 2009 Pro Bowl in Hawaii.

Peterson scored his final college touchdown against Boise State in the 2007 Fiesta Bowl.

Peterson was a dominant running back. It seemed he could only be slowed down by injuries. He injured his ankle in the 2005 season-opener. But he was back for the second game. He exploded for 220 yards. But Peterson fell into the first slump of his career after that. He hit rock bottom against the University of Kansas that October. He carried the ball five times but rushed for minus-four yards.

Peterson remained close with his dad while Nelson was in prison. Nelson was released in October 2006. He even came to one of his son's games that year. Peterson was thrilled. But it happened to be the game in which he broke his collarbone.

The ankle injury still bothered Peterson. He had to miss the next game. But Oklahoma played the University of Nebraska after that. They were conference rivals. Peterson was back for that game. He rushed for 146 yards and two touchdowns. That helped Oklahoma get an important victory. Peterson had to play through pain to help his team that day.

Peterson added three more 100-yard performances that season. He peaked with a 237-yard game against Oklahoma State. But he would never repeat his freshman success. A collarbone injury forced him to miss seven games as a junior. Peterson rushed for a combined 2,120 yards as a sophomore and junior. That was only about 200 yards more than what he gained as a freshman. His college career ended in disappointment when Boise State University upset the Sooners in the 2007 Fiesta Bowl.

Still, when healthy, Peterson was one of the nation's best players. So he decided to enter the NFL Draft after that junior season. It was supposed to be a fun and exciting time. Peterson was expected to be a high draft pick. But it turned out to be a sad time for Peterson. His half-brother Chris Paris was shot and killed just weeks before the draft. Peterson had spoken with Chris a few days earlier.

Like before, Peterson did not let tragedy slow him down. He said football helped him deal with the pain. That helped motivate Peterson as he worked out for NFL teams.

Few doubted that Peterson was really good. But some NFL teams worried about his injury history. They did not want to select a player who got injured a lot. The Minnesota Vikings were not one of those teams. They selected him with the seventh pick in the 2007 NFL Draft. Six teams passed on Peterson. He would soon make them wish they had not.

Peterson poses with NFL commissioner Roger Goodell after the Minnesota Vikings selected Peterson in the 2007 NFL Draft.

Adrian Peterson

CHAPTER 3

VICTORIES WITH THE VIKINGS

Adrian Peterson made an early impact at the college level. He excelled from the start for the Vikings too. His first big NFL game came against the Chicago Bears. Peterson had a team-record 224 yards. He also scored three touchdowns. A few weeks later he racked up an NFL-record 296 rushing yards against the San Diego Chargers.

Fans around the NFL were excited to see Peterson's success. He did not play like a rookie.

Peterson scored his first NFL rushing touchdown against the Kansas City Chiefs.

Some people were already comparing him to the league's all-time greats. Peterson had great vision on the field. He was also very powerful. Those qualities made him a force. Defensive players were supposed to tackle Peterson. Instead, he just ran right through them!

Peterson was able to do things that year that no rookie had ever done before. He finished his rookie season with 1,341 yards and 12 touchdowns. Only one player bested him in those categories. Peterson's effort landed him a spot in the Pro Bowl. That is the NFL's All-Star game. Peterson capped off the season by being named the Pro Bowl's Most Valuable Player.

After Peterson's rookie season, teams knew what to expect. The Vikings were not a great passing team. So defenses could focus more on stopping Peterson. But even that did little to slow him down. Peterson became the finest running back in the NFL in 2008. He led the league with 1,760 rushing yards. Only one second-year player had ever rushed for more yards at the time.

Peterson also rushed for more than 100 yards in 10 of his 16 games. Vikings fans were especially happy about one of

Peterson rushed for three touchdowns against the Chicago Bears in his fifth NFL game.

those performances. The Vikings were playing the rival Green Bay Packers at home in the Metrodome. The Packers had the lead with time ticking away. But the Vikings got the ball back. Peterson took over from there. He racked up 40 rushing yards and 24 receiving yards on the drive. He capped it off with a touchdown. The Vikings held on for a 28–27 win. Peterson had 192 total rushing yards in the game.

Minnesota had won six games in the season before Peterson arrived. In Peterson's rookie year, the Vikings won eight games. Peterson then led them to 10 victories in his second year. Minnesota also reached the playoffs for the first time in four years in 2008. But the playoffs did not go as Peterson and the Vikings had hoped. The Vikings struggled passing the ball against the Philadelphia Eagles. That allowed the Eagles to focus more on Peterson. He still rushed for 83 yards and two touchdowns. However, the Vikings lost.

Peterson had become a force in the NFL. He had also become known for his charity work. Peterson volunteered for Special Olympics Minnesota. That organization provided an athletic outlet for people with physical disabilities. Peterson worked with the African American Adoption Agency and the Make-A-Wish Foundation too.

The NFL Players Association gave Peterson its "Emerging Leader" award in April 2008. It recognized his work with several charitable organizations.

Peterson breaks away from the Philadelphia Eagles' defense for a 40-yard touchdown run in his first playoff game.

Peterson's off-the-field work was only beginning. He was most interested in helping children. He soon launched the Adrian Peterson All Day Foundation. It raises money and support for the Boys and Girls Club of the Twin Cities and other charities. Peterson was doing great things. But he and the Vikings still had plenty of work left to do on the football field as well.

Adrian Peterson

CHAPTER 4

A NEW ERA

Adrian Peterson was just one of many returning stars coming back for the 2009 season. And the Vikings saw an opportunity to possibly win their first Super Bowl. So they signed legendary quarterback Brett Favre to guide them.

It turned out Favre was just what they needed. The Vikings improved both on offense and defense. They sprinted out to a 10–1 start. And Peterson led the team with 1,383 rushing yards on the season.

Peterson takes a handoff from quarterback Brett Favre during the 2009 season.

He also scored 18 touchdowns. That was more than any NFL player that year.

Minnesota finished the regular season at 12–4. That earned the Vikings a first-round bye in the playoffs. Minnesota dominated the visiting Dallas Cowboys in the second round. That set up a conference title showdown against the New Orleans Saints.

The Super Bowl was in reach. But it would not be easy. The Saints had finished the season with the best record in the conference. So the Vikings had to travel to New Orleans for the game. It was a hard place to play. But Peterson and the Vikings came out hard.

Peterson rushed for 122 yards in the game. He also scored three touchdowns. His last score tied the game in the fourth quarter. But the Saints won it on a field goal in overtime.

The NFL Network ranked the league's top 100 players in 2011. The players themselves cast the votes. Peterson finished third in the voting. Only quarterbacks Tom Brady and Peyton Manning were ranked ahead of him.

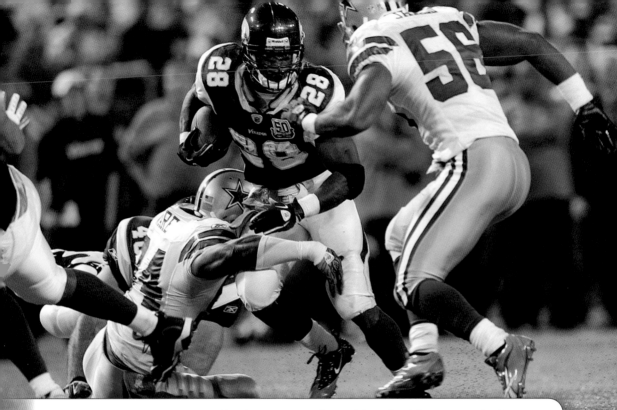

Peterson reached 5,000 yards rushing for his career during the 2010 season.

Turnovers played a big role in the Vikings' loss. Favre threw two interceptions. The Vikings also fumbled the ball six times. The Saints recovered three of those fumbles. Two of the team's fumbles came from Peterson. The Vikings got the ball back both of those times. But Peterson was crushed.

Peterson and the Vikings had high hopes for 2010. Many of the players from the 2009 team were back. They thought they might finally win the Super Bowl that year. Peterson was still a top running back in 2010. But his team was no longer one of the best. It did not seem to matter how well Peterson performed. He rushed for 1,298 yards. He scored 12 touchdowns and only fumbled once all season. He continued to shine despite hurting his ankle in late November. And he was named to the Pro Bowl for the fourth season in a row.

Yet the Vikings still finished with just a 6–10 record. They lost five of their first seven games. That proved too hard to come back from. Minnesota never even threatened to reach the playoffs. The team finished last in its division. It was a hard season for Peterson. He was not used to losing that much.

The Vikings' rough 2010 season did not stop Peterson from his off-field mission, though. One of his passions became helping the poor people of Africa. Millions of people there suffer from the effects of war, starvation, and disease. In March

Peterson missed a few days of training camp before the 2011 season when his fiancée gave birth to Adrian Peterson Jr. That was Peterson's first son. He also has a daughter named Adeja.

Peterson and the Vikings signed a contract in 2011 to keep him in Minnesota for at least seven more seasons.

2010, Peterson and several other NFL players traveled to Uganda and Rwanda as part of the "Pros for Africa" program.

Peterson put the 2010 season behind him and looked toward the future. The Vikings offered him a new contract before the 2011 season. It said Peterson would remain in Minnesota for at least seven more years. That is a lot of time to break more records and win a Super Bowl!

FUN FACTS AND QUOTES

- Adrian Peterson and his mother Bonita Jackson were not the only fine athletes in the family. His uncle, Ivory Lee Brown, played one season for the NFL's Phoenix Cardinals. Like his nephew, Brown also played running back. He rushed for 194 yards and two touchdowns in 1992. Peterson's father, Nelson, played college basketball at Idaho State University.

- The love Peterson kept in his heart for his late brother Brian remained apparent in his NFL career. After he snagged a 60-yard pass and ran it into the end zone for a touchdown in his first NFL regular season game, Peterson blew a kiss to the sky to honor his departed brother.

- A couple was visiting Las Vegas, Nevada, in spring of 2010 when they saw Peterson. They asked if it was indeed him. He confirmed it was. Then he invited the couple and about a dozen others to join him for dinner. Peterson paid for the $400 spread.

- "If I could play any other position, it would be safety. Sometimes I just want to hit somebody. One of these days you're going to see me as the [lead tackler] on special teams. You watch."—*Peterson before the 2009 season opener against the Cleveland Browns*

WEB LINKS

To learn more about Adrian Peterson, visit ABDO Publishing Company online at **www.abdopublishing.com**. Web sites about Peterson are featured on our Book Links page. These links are routinely monitored and updated to provide the most current information available.

GLOSSARY

bye
A week in which a team has no scheduled game. The top teams in the regular season earn byes in the first round of the playoffs.

charity
Money given or work done to help people in need.

draft
An annual event in which NFL teams select the top college football players.

drive
A sustained movement downfield by the offensive football team.

fumble
When a player loses possession of the ball.

overtime
An extra session of football played when a game is tied after four regulation periods.

recruiters
People who are trying to convince high school football players to play for their colleges.

rival
An opponent that brings out great emotion in a team, its fans, and its players.

rookie
A first-year player in the NFL.

scholarship
Financial assistance awarded to students to help them pay for school. Top athletes earn scholarships to represent a college through its sports teams.

scout
A talent evaluator for a college athletic program or professional sports team often responsible for signing prospective players.

INDEX

FURTHER RESOURCES

Fletcher, Jim. *The Die-Hard Fan's Guide to Sooner Football*. Washington DC: Regnery Pub., 2008.

Gitlin, Marty. *Minnesota Vikings*. Edina, MN: ABDO Publishing Co., 2011.

Reusse, Patrick. *Minnesota Vikings: The Complete Illustrated History*. Minneapolis: MVP Books, 2010.